MW00446133

*This book is dedicated to my husband, my sweet baby boy, and my supportive family and friends who encourage me everyday to be my authentic self.*

# Smoothies
## & Smoothie Popsicles

# For Toddlers and Kids

### by Leslie Osborne
### with Allison Belt

# Contents

# Introduction

One morning, like so many other mornings, I needed to make breakfast for myself and my ten month old son, who had been eating "solids" for a few months. I usually look to smoothies as my go-to breakfast when I want something quick and healthy, and I was pleasantly surprised to realize that all the ingredients in my smoothie were foods that my son had already been introduced to. I made a little extra for him and he absolutely loved it!

Wonder of wonders, I was able to feed us both a nutritious, satisfying breakfast at the same time. In that moment I knew I wanted to create smoothie recipes for families that struggle to feed themselves and their little ones REAL food. And so Smoothies and Smoothie Popsicles for Toddlers and Kids was born!

Here's the thing: technology has given us many gifts, gifts that save lives and connect humans and further our growth. But there's not a lot that technology has given us that's made feeding kids easier.

Especially feeding kids nutritious, filling, gratifying food. However, there is one piece of equipment that has redeemed the sometimes arduous task of feeding my toddler well, and that, my friends, is my blender.

Yes. My blender.

I can throw some of my son's favorite things (bananas, peanut butter, dates) along with some of his least favorite things (kale, flax seeds, raw oats) in this amazing machine, push a button, and a minute later I have a treat/snack/meal for him that he gulps down with gusto.

Thank you, science.

I have put together fourteen of my favorite recipes. My goal was that they would not only be delicious and full of good fats, hearty proteins, fortifying vitamins, and immune-boosting antioxidants, but that would also be easy to make with ingredients you can find at your local grocery store or farmers' market. I truly believe that it's possible to feed a child well without breaking the bank.

I'm confident your kids are going to LOVE these smoothies... and YOU will too!

So here you go, friends. Enjoy and bon appétit ya'll!

Leslie

SUPERFOOD
*Ingredients*

# INGREDIENTS & RESOURCES

# Ingredients

We believe that the key to any successful smoothie–to any successful recipe–is having the best ingredients. Below is a list of those ingredients that show up the most in this book and a few notes on how to maximize their flavor and nutritional benefits.

**Cocoa Powder** – the harvesting and processing of cocoa powder are ethically iffy in the best of circumstances. We encourage you to spend the extra money to buy fair-trade cocoa products. They taste far superior and that extra money goes to supporting small farmers with sustainable practices.

**Coconut Oil** – we use cold-pressed, extra virgin coconut oil because it's excellent for brain health and healing on so many levels.

**Coconut Milk** – whenever we call for coconut milk, know that we're using the unsweetened, full fat coconut milk you find in a can, not the refrigerated milk alternative. Full fat coconut milk makes smoothies that have the ice-creaminess kids love without the dairy. In the popsicle recipes, it's substituted for all other milk alternatives (with a couple of exceptions) to cut down on crystallization.

**Dates** – we use Medjool dates in our recipes because they naturally add sweetness along with some great fiber.

**Flax seeds** – we encourage you to buy whole flax seeds instead of ground and let the action of the blender do the grinding blender do the grinding. Pre-ground flax seeds go rancid pretty quickly, which takes away from the nuttiness they bring to a recipe.

**Fresh versus Frozen Fruits** – ideally any fruit you use in these recipes would be organic, local, and in-season. Ideally. Knowing that's not often the case, we use organic, frozen fruits that we've put up ourselves or bought at our local grocer. Conventional fruit production is rife with pesticide use, so it's vitally important to use organic fruit whenever and wherever possible.

**Nut Butters** – we use both almond butter and peanut butter in the following recipes, and for both products we choose brands that use only the ground nut and with maybe a touch of oil or salt, but no added sugar.

**Nut Milks** – the recipes alternate between almond and cashew milks, and while both are able to be substituted in any recipe, the almond milk will add a nuttiness, while the cashew milk has a cleaner flavor.

**Tofu** – we use fermented, organic, silken tofu to add a creamy thickness and a bit of protein, but for those who don't do soy products, it can be omitted.

**Yogurt** – the more fat in a plain or Greek yogurt, the less sugar there is, so we use full fat/whole milk yogurt (sometimes with a touch of vanilla) in the following recipes.

**Kale** – we used kale as the only green in our green smoothies as it has a neutral flavor, but is a powerhouse in the nutrient department!

# Equipment

The other key to a successful recipe is having great equipment. Here are some of our favorites.

**Blender/Vitamix** – these recipes were developed using a BlendTech blender, though any blender will do. Some smaller models (like the Bullet) may not hold all the ingredients called for, in which case the recipes may need to be halved.

**Popsicle Molds** – we tried a number of different molds, and these that we got at Target were the most durable and the least expensive!

**Citrus Zester** – a good citrus zester is one of those things you don't know you need until you get one. Then you can't live without it!

**Squeeze pouches** – if your baby or toddler doesn't quite have the hang of drinking out of a cup or straw, these pouches are ideal. They're reusable and resealable and can be taken on-the-go for easy snacks. They can be filled with applesauce and yogurt as well as smoothies, so you really get a lot of use out of them. They are also really easy to clean as you don't have to worry about hard-to-clean straws. You can find these on amazon.com or squooshi.com.

# SMOOTHIE POPSICLES!

# A note about pops!

Some of these recipes make incredible pops for your kids, which means you can make them ahead and have them ready on those hot summer afternoons. Most of our recipes make 16 to 24 ounces of smoothie, and most popsicle molds make 3-5 ounce pops, which means you get a lot of bang for your buck when you opt for a pop! We've added our favorite popsicle mold in our instrument list.

The key to a good pop is that it is creamy and not too icy, so we've given you some tips for that. In converting most of the recipes from a smoothie to a pop you generally want to substitute coconut milk (preferably full fat) in place of any other nut milk called for, with a couple of exceptions. And you definitely want to omit ice cubes, as they will cause some intense crystallization. Lastly, we suggest adding a pinch of xanthan gum, cornstarch, or tapioca starch, all of which you can get at your local health food store or most grocery stores. It will cut down on crystallization without affecting the taste! Not all of the recipes convert to popsicles because it would require more sugar to be added to bring out their flavor, which we didn't want.

# A note about prep!

For the most part, the dry ingredients for these recipes can be thrown together in a Ziploc bag and stuck in your freezer until you're ready to put them in the blender with the wet ingredients. This cuts down on an already incredibly low prep time. This is especially great if you, like me, by your fruit in bulk. When I have a glut of mangoes (I often find them on sale 10 for $10) I cut them up and put them in little individual Ziplocs, and maybe throw in a sliver of ginger with them. The next week I buy pineapple in bulk and throw some chunks and core in the Ziploc with the mango. The next week my mint comes in my garden and I throw my frozen bag of mango, pineapple, and ginger in the blender, add the mint and a little water, and I have my Mango Pineapple Ginger Smoothie (see page 34-35).

You can also freeze kale if you, like me, are drowning in it in the summertime and craving it in winter or can only buy it in extra large bags at the store and don't want it to go to waste. This ensures you have high quality greens in your beautiful green smoothies year round.  Also, if you have extra bananas that you don't want to go bad, you can remove the skins, and freeze them too!

# How to get the best flavor and texture!

**Fresh Fruit** - This might seem like a no-brainer, but always remember to use **RIPE** fruit! If your fresh fruit isn't quite ripe enough, your smoothies will have a "flat" flavor. The more ripe your fruit is, the naturally sweeter it will be. We all know bananas don't taste good when they are green. The same goes for any other fruit. Kiwis are really tart and don't have much flavor, mangoes aren't as soft and sweet, and peaches don't have that succulent sweet peach goodness when they are underripe. If you want to make a smoothie with less-ripe fruit, you might need to add a little honey to enhance their natural sweetness.

**Blending Smoothies** - Depending on what kind of blender you have, you may need to blend certain smoothies a little longer to acheive a smooth texture. Any smoothies with kale may need to blend for a full 2-4 minutes to ensure they are really smooth. You will still have the tiniest particles of kale, but they will still taste great. If texture is a big issue with your kids, just blend a bit more!

# RECIPES

LEMONY
*Blueberry*
PEACH
*Oatmeal*

# Lemony Blueberry Peach Oatmeal & Pops

This smoothie pairs the warmth of nutty, filling oats with the tang of sweet peaches and blueberries. It's the perfect blend of bright, savory and sweet, and it's full of calcium, good fats, and antioxidants. The popsicle version is so refreshing on a summer day!

| | |
|---:|:---|
| $3/_4$ *cup* | blueberries, fresh or frozen |
| 2 | peaches, fresh or frozen (about 1 heaping cup) |
| | |
| $3/_4$ *cup* | yogurt |
| $1/_4$ *cup* | oats |
| *1 cup* | coconut milk or almond milk |
| *1* | lemon zested |
| **For Pops** | add one of the following 3: |
| $1/_8$ *teaspoon* | xanthan gum |
| $1/_4$ *teaspoon* | cornstarch or tapioca starch |

1. Puree all ingredients until very smooth. Alternatively, add the yogurt, lemon zest, and coconut or almond milk in the blender with the oats and let them soak over night (it helps soften the oats and the lemon infuses throughout the ingredients). Add the fruit and blend in the morning.

2. For the pops: Use coconut milk for a creamier texture and add either xanthan gum, cornstarch, or tapioca starch to the smoothie. Stir and pour in cold popsicle molds and freeze.

# Strawberry
# LEMONADE
# Kale
# PEACH

# Strawberry Lemonade/Kale Peach Duo

This smoothie is truly a showstopper, whether in a glass or in pop form. The Strawberry Lemonade is everything you want it to be, and the Kale Peach portion adds a tropical and creamy flavor that really sets this smoothie apart. On their own they are good, but together they're magic!

### Strawberry Lemonade

- **1 cup** strawberries (preferably frozen)
- **1 cup** water
- **1** lemon, juiced and zested
- **3 teaspoons** honey
- **Sliver** fresh ginger
- **2-3** ice cubes (if using all fresh fruit)

### Kale Peach Layer

- **1 cup** kale
- **1 cup** peaches (preferably frozen)
- **³/₄ cup** coconut milk
- **1 squeeze** lemon plus some zest from lemon above
- **1 teaspoon** honey
- **Sliver** fresh ginger
- **2** ice cubes (if using all fresh fruit)

1. Blend the ingredients for the strawberry lemonade, pour into two glasses, and place in the freezer while making the kale peach. Make sure and rinse your blender in cold water.

2. Blend the ingredients for the kale peach REALLY WELL until nice and smooth, and top the strawberry lemonade. The sweetness may need to be adjusted depending on the sweetness of your strawberries. Serve immediately (it can keep in the freezer for about 30 minutes, but don't let it freeze completely)!

3. Pop Variation: Omit the ices and reverse the order! The Kale Peach will be poured into your popsicle molds first, followed by the Strawberry Lemonade! Only pour in a small amount of the Kale Peach, let it firm for a few minutes in the freezer, followed by the strawberry as you want mostly Strawberry Lemonade in the pops.

4. This recipe doesn't need any xanthan gum, cornstarch, or tapioca starch as the honey reduces ice crystals.

Kale
Pineapple
Peach

# Kale Pineapple Peach

The tofu in this smoothie is completely flavorless, and it adds creaminess and about 4 grams of protein! The flavor is refreshing and has a tropical vibe. If you use fresh fruit instead of frozen, add a few ice cubes to the smoothie to ensure it's nice and cold.

| | |
|---:|---|
| *1 handful* | kale |
| *1 cup* | pineapple (use core if available for added nutrition) |
| *1 cup* | fresh or frozen sliced peaches |
| *$1/_2$ cup* | vanilla or Greek yogurt (packs a protein punch!) |
| *1 cup* | cold water |
| *$1/_4$ cup* | organic silken tofu |
| *Sliver* | fresh ginger |
| *2 or 3* | ice cubes if using fresh fruit |

1. Blend all ingredients until smooth. Depending on your blender, this recipe might require up 3-4 minutes of blending to ensure better texture. Makes 24 ounces, or two large servings. This is best as a smoothie only.

2. Fresh or frozen mango can be substituted for pineapple.

# Kale
# Kiwi
# Smoothie

# Kale Kiwi Smoothie

Green! Green! Green! Between the kale and the kiwi, this smoothie might be the greenest one I've ever seen. But rest assured, any "earthiness" from the kale that your little one might be wary of is silenced by the sweetly tart and complex kiwi flavors. Needless to say, this smoothie is chock full of antioxidants and fiber!

| | |
|---:|:---|
| *1 cup* | kale (preferably chopped) |
| *1 ¹/₂ cups* | cashew milk |
| *1* | banana |
| *3* | kiwis, peeled |

1. Blend the kale, banana, and nut milk together until REALLY smooth. This may take 3-4 minutes, depending on your blender.  Then, on LOW speed add the kiwis until they are just blended. You want to make sure the seeds are mostly intact, otherwise the texture changes dramatically!

2. This smoothie tastes best just as a smoothie, and not as a popsicle.

# Mango
## PINEAPPLE
### Ginger

# Mango Pineapple Ginger Smoothie

This smoothie is a real fighter. With ginger and mint and pineapple core (a nutrient-dense part of the pineapple that's often overlooked), this smoothie turns out to not only be incredibly refreshing, but it also supports the immune system!

| | |
|---:|---|
| *1* | ripe mango (fresh or frozen) |
| *3/4 cup* | pineapple, with core |
| *3 sprigs* | fresh mint |
| *small handful* | kale |
| *1/2 inch* | sliver fresh ginger |
| *1 cup* | cold water |
| *3-4* | ice cubes if using fresh fruit |

1.  Blend all ingredients together until smooth.  So refreshing, AHHHH!
2.  This smoothie is best as a smoothie only.

*Berry*
# GOOD
*Greens*

# Berry Good Greens

This smoothie blends the creaminess of the tofu and almond milk with the tang of ginger, and what happens is pretty incredible.

| | |
|---:|:---|
| *1 cup* | blueberries, fresh or frozen |
| *1 cup* | mango, fresh or frozen |
| *1 1/2 cups* | almond milk |
| *1/4 cup* | organic silken tofu (optional) |
| *1/2 cup* | kale, firmly packed |
| *Sliver* | fresh ginger |
| *1 teaspoon* | honey (if mango isn't very sweet) |
| *3-4* | ice cubes if using fresh fruit |

1. Blend ingredients until smooth. Enjoy! It's best as a smoothie only.

# CHOCOLATE
## *Peanut Butter*
# PRETZEL

# Chocolate Peanut Butter Pretzel Smoothie

This smoothie is absolutely decadent and has the perfect balance of savory and sweet. It's like having a peanut butter cup in a creamy, milky form, but without the loads of sugar. The avocado adds smoothness and a dose of healthy fats, while the flax seeds add nuttiness and omega-3! Making your own chocolate-dipped pretzels will take no time, and there will be far fewer calories than the store-bought ones.

$^1/_2$ avocado

$1\,^1/_2$ **cups** almond or cashew milk

$^1/_2$ **cup** peanut butter or almond butter

2 **tablespoons** cocoa powder

$^1/_2$ **teaspoon** flax seeds (optional)

$^1/_4$ **cup** pretzels (or gluten free pretzels)

$^1/_4$ **cup** bittersweet chocolate chips

5 ice cubes

**For the pops** add one of the following:

$^1/_8$ **teaspoon** xanthan gum or

$^1/_4$ **teaspoon** cornstarch or tapioca starch

1.  Heat the chocolate chips in a bowl in the microwave for 10 second intervals until most of the chips are melted. A double-boiler on the stovetop also works! Stir to finish melting. Dip the pretzels into the chocolate and set aside. They can be placed in the freezer for a couple of minutes to set up while you get your other ingredients together, but take out when the chocolate is set. Add all other ingredients to your blender, including all but a few of the pretzels, and blend until smooth. Garnish with extra chocolate pretzels.

2.  Pop Variation: Use coconut milk instead of almond milk for a creamier texture, omit ice cubes, blend all of the chocolate pretzels, and add xanthan gum, cornstarch, or tapioca starch.

3.  *If the smoothie is too thick for you or your child's liking, just add a bit more liquid.

Chocolate
BANANA
Pistachio

# Chocolate Banana Pistachio

This Chocolate Banana Pistachio smoothie is stunningly perfect. It's low in sugar and high in good fats, and the toasted coconut chips make it decadent! If your toddler loves chocolate milk, she'll love this smoothie.

| | |
|---:|:---|
| *1* | banana (fresh or frozen) |
| *1/4 cup* | pistachios |
| *1 cup* | almond or coconut milk |
| *3 tablespoons* | toasted coconut chips (optional) |
| *2 1/2 tablespoons* | cocoa powder |
| *1* | Medjool date, pitted |
| *1/4 teaspoon* | vanilla |
| *1/4 teaspoon* | cinnamon |
| *1/2 teaspoon* | coconut oil (optional) |
| *5* | ice cubes if using fresh banana |
| *For the Pops* | add one of the following: |
| *1/8 teaspoon* | xanthan gum or |
| *1/4 teaspoon* | cornstarch or tapioca starch |

1. Blend all the ingredients together until smooth.
2. For pops: Omit ice cubes if making pops. Add either xanthan gum, cornstarch, or tapioca starch, stir and freeze.

# Peanut Butter

# &

# Jelly

# Peanut Butter & Jelly Smoothie

Okay, so not only is this smoothie packed with protein, it's also beautiful with its swirl of jelly at the end. It will keep your kiddo (and you!) fuller longer without the sugar crash of a real PB&J. And it tastes like the most decadent peanut butter ice cream.

| | |
|---:|:---|
| $1/_3$ **cup** | peanut butter (brands with peanuts and salt only) |
| $1/_2$ **cup** | vanilla or Greek yogurt |
| *1* | banana (preferably frozen) |
| $1/_2$ **cup** | almond, cashew, or regular milk |
| *4* | ice cubes (if using fresh banana) |
| **2 teaspoons** | strawberry or raspberry jam for swirling |
| **For the Pops** | add one of the following: |
| $1/_8$ **teaspoon** | xanthan gum or |
| $1/_4$ **teaspoon** | cornstarch or tapioca starch |

1. Blend all ingredients except jam until smooth. Swirl 1 teaspoon of jam around the inside of two glasses and pour in smoothie mixture. This makes 16 ounces, but it's so rich it's perfect as two 8 ounce servings!

2. For the pops: Don't add ice cubes. Regular dairy milk works best for the pops. Stir in either xanthan gum, cornstarch, or tapioca starch into the smoothie. Swirl jam inside the popsicle molds, pour in the smoothie mixture and freeze!

# Oatmeal
## COOKIE
## Dough

# Oatmeal Cookie Dough

This smoothie is nutty and creamy and filling. The key to using raw oats in a recipe is soaking them for at least two hours, if not overnight. We suggest you soak the oats and the flax seeds in the cashew milk that's called for in the recipe. There's enough water content in the milk to break down the phytic acid, and it cuts down on the already minimal steps!

| | |
|---:|:---|
| $^1/_2$ *cup* | oats |
| *1 cup* | cashew milk or almond milk |
| $^1/_2$ *teaspoon* | flax seeds |
| *1* | banana (fresh or frozen) |
| $^1/_3$ *cup* | almond butter |
| *1* | Medjool date, pitted |
| *1 $^1/_2$ teaspoon* | honey |
| *5* | ice cubes if using fresh banana |
| *For the Pops* | add one of the following |
| $^1/_8$ *teaspoon* | xanthan gum |
| $^1/_4$ *teaspoon* | cornstarch or tapioca starch |

1. Add oats and flax seeds to the blender and soak in the cashew milk for at least 2 hours or overnight. Place in the fridge. Add the rest of the ingredients in the morning and blend. This is also a great afternoon snack! *You can opt not to soak the oats and flax if you are short on time, but it aids digestion if you do soak them.

2. For the pops: Omit the ice cubes and use cashew milk since it's richer in flavor. Stir in either xanthan gum, cornstarch, or tapioca starch. Pour in popsicle molds and freeze!

Cheesecake
Smoothie

# Cheesecake Smoothie

It's hard to say if this smoothie is for the kids or for the parents. The cashews add protein and creaminess, as does the yogurt (Greek yogurt especially!). You'll want to soak the cashews overnight in water to soften. If you haven't worked with blended raw cashews yet, get ready. They'll change your world.

| | |
|---:|---|
| *1* | banana (fresh or frozen) |
| *¹/₂ cup* | vanilla yogurt or Greek yogurt |
| *1 cup* | coconut milk |
| *¹/₄ cup* | cashews, soaked |
| *1 cup* | pitted medjool date |
| *¹/₄ teaspoon* | vanilla |
| *¹/₂ teaspoon* | coconut oil (optional) |
| *5* | ice cubes if using fresh banana |

1. Soak cashews for at least two hours or overnight in water to soften. Rinse and drain and add to the blender. Add all ingredients and blend. Tastes like liquid cheesecake!

2. This tastes best as a smoothie only.

# Banana BREAD Smoothie

# Banana Bread Smoothie

The secret here is the orange zest. It brightens up the smoothie and intensifies all the other flavors. The toasted pecans, flax seeds, and coconut oil are great sources of healthy fats, while cinnamon is touted for its anti-inflammatory properties. But above and beyond that, this smoothie brings all the comfort of freshly baked banana bread without all the sugar.

| | |
|---:|:---|
| *1* | banana (fresh or frozen) |
| $1/_4$ *cup* | toasted pecans |
| $1/_8$ *teaspoon* | cinnamon |
| *1* $1/_2$ *cups* | cashew or almond milk |
| $1/_2$ *teaspoon* | flax seeds |
| $1/_2$ *teaspoon* | coconut oil (optional) |
| $1/_2$ *teaspoon* | orange zest (don't skip, so good!) |
| *3 tablespoon* | almond butter |
| *5* | ice cubes if using fresh banana |
| *For the Pops* | add one of the following: |
| $1/_8$ *teaspoon* | xanthan gum or |
| $1/_4$ *teaspoon* | cornstarch or tapioca starch |

1. Blend all ingredients and enjoy!

2. Pop Variation: Coconut milk will overwhelm the other flavors so stick with cashew or almond milk. Omit ice cubes, and add xanthan gum, cornstarch, or tapioca starch.

# Avocado
# KEY LIME
# Pudding

# Key Lime Avocado Pudding & Pops

There's something a little bit sophisticated about this key lime pop. The tang of the limes balances the creaminess of the yogurt and coconut milk and the balance is something adults can enjoy while the kids are munching away.

| | |
|---:|:---|
| 1 | ripe avocado |
| 1 cup | coconut milk |
| 2 | limes zested and juiced |
| 3 teaspoon | honey |
| 1/4 cup | vanilla or plain yogurt |
| 1/2 teaspoon | coconut oil (optional) |

| | |
|---:|:---|
| For the Pops | add one of the following: |
| 1/8 teaspoon | xanthan gum or |
| 1/4 teaspoon | cornstarch or tapioca starch |

1. You definitely want to use full fat, unsweetened coconut milk because it sets up better in pops and has a less icy texture. Blend all ingredients together. If your kids love tart flavors, add the juice of both the limes instead of one and a half. You can also refrigerate the mixture and serve as a pudding snack or dessert with crushed ginger snaps. This will stay fresh in the fridge for 24 hours.

2. While the honey will cut down on crystallization, adding xanthan gum, cornstarch, or tapioca will make it even creamier!

Pumpkin
PIE
Smoothie

# Pumpkin Pie Smoothie & Pops

That's right. Pumpkin Pie Smoothie. And it is amazing. The subtle spices in this recipe are full of great antioxidants, but they don't overpower, and they might even expand the horizons of your little one's palate. There are also some great fats, and the pumpkin adds fiber, which isn't always easy to get in a child's diet.

| | |
|---|---|
| *1 cup plus 2 tablespoons* | pure canned pumpkin |
| *¹/₂ teaspoon* | cinnamon* |
| *¹/₄ teaspoon* | nutmeg* |
| *¹/₈ teaspoon* | cloves* |
| *1 pinch* | ground ginger* |
| *1* | banana |
| *¹/₂ cup* | yogurt |
| *¹/₂ cup* | coconut, cashew or almond milk |
| | |
| *For the Pops* | add 1 of the following: |
| *¹/₈ teaspoon* | xanthan gum or |
| *¹/₄ teaspoon* | cornstarch or tapioca starch |

1. Blend all ingredients until smooth.
2. *Instead of adding all these ingredients individually, you can add just under 1 teaspoon of pumpkin pie spice.
3. For the pops: Use coconut milk and add xanthan gum, cornstarch, or tapioca starch to the smoothie. Stir and pour into cold popsicle molds and freeze.

# About the Author

Leslie Osborne has always been passionate about cooking, so much so that she pursued a life-long dream of attending culinary school in 2012 at The French Pastry School in Chicago, IL. She completed the intensive two month artisan bread-baking course and fell in love with baking old-world breads and pastries. After the birth of her son in 2014, she wanted to keep her feet in the culinary world, but didn't want to work the grueling hours of a bakery. Instead, she started her own food blog called <u>Bessie Bakes</u> where she could share whole foods recipes and artisan baked goods with anyone looking to make some mouth-watering food.

As a result of starting a food blog, she has been enjoying diving into food photography and taking pictures of all the yummy smoothies in this book. Of course her son has been the inspiration for this book that has become a labor of love. He loves drinking smoothies (he calls them "moothies") and got to be the chief taste-tester for all the recipes in this book. Her wish is for all children to be nourished with healthy whole foods so they can thrive and live fulfilling lives.

## Copyright

All contents copyright © *2016* by *Leslie Osborne*. All rights reserved. No part of this document may be reproduced or transmitted in any form, by any means (electronic, photocopying, recording, or otherwise) without the prior written permission of the publisher.

## Sharing this Document

There was a lot of work that went into putting this cookbook together. I can't tell you how many countless hours are spent putting together the *Bessie Bakes* blog from which this information was compiled. That means that this information has value, and your friends, neighbors, and co-workers may want to share it.

The information in this document is copyrighted. I would ask that you do not share this information with others - you alone have the rights to use this book. Any person who has not purchased and downloaded this book from the *Bessie Bakes* website or any other sites that have been given permission to sell this book does not have that right. Sharing it without my permission is considered copyright infringement.

It should go without saying that you cannot post this document or the information it contains on any electronic bulletin board, Web site, FTP site, newsgroup, or anywhere else. Thank you for downloading this cookbook. I hope you find the information useful and delicious. Your support means the world!

# Follow "Bessie Bakes"

Subscribe to the blog and receive a FREE ebook *"Dairy Free Homemade Nut Milks"*!

You'll get **3** super delicious recipes and learn the most **ingenious** way to strain them!

Learn more at bessiebakes.com

*Bon Appétit Ya'll,*
*Leslie Osborne*

40877829R00038

Made in the USA
San Bernardino, CA
30 October 2016